# REQUIEM:
# FOR THE INNOCENTS

*And Other Poems*

# BENSON BOBRICK

ANAPHORA LITERARY PRESS

DICKINSON, NORTH DAKOTA

ANAPHORA LITERARY PRESS
1053 Koch Street, #210
Dickinson, ND 58601
https://anaphoraliterary.com

**Book design by Anna Faktorovich, Ph.D.**

Printed in the United States of America, United Kingdom and in Australia on acid-free paper.

Cover Images: "Border", 18th century. Gift of David Adler: Art Institute of Chicago.
"Decorated Initial "B" with Border, probably copied from a Psalter in the British Library", 1890-1930. The Art Institute of Chicago.

Published in 2026 by Anaphora Literary Press

Requiem: For the Innocents: And Other Poems
Benson Bobrick—1st edition.

Library of Congress Control Number: 2026902564

**Library Cataloging Information**
Bobrick, Benson, 1947-, author.
    Requiem : For the innocents : And other poems / Benson Bobrick
    80 p. ; 9 in.
    ISBN 978-1-68114-631-7 (softcover : alk. paper)
    ISBN 978-1-68114-632-4 (hardcover : alk. paper)
    Amazon Kindle ASIN (e-book)
1. Books—Literature & Fiction—Poetry—United States—General.
2. Books—Literature & Fiction—Poetry—Single Authors.
3. Books—Literature & Fiction—Poetry—Love Poems.
PN6099-6110: Collections of general literature: Poetry
811: American poetry in English

# ALSO BY BENSON BOBRICK

*Labyrinths of Iron:*
*Subways in History, Myth, Art, Technology, & War*

*Parsons Brinckerhoff: The First Hundred Years*

*Fearful Majesty: The Life and Reign of Ivan the Terrible*

*East of the Sun: The Epic Conquest and Tragic History of Siberia*

*Knotted Tongues: Stuttering in History and the Quest for a Cure*

*Angel in the Whirlwind: The Triumph of the American Revolution*

*Wide as the Waters: The Story of the English Bible*
*and the Revolution It Inspired*

*Testament: A Soldier's Story of the Civil War*

*The Fated Sky: Astrology in History*

*Master of War: The Life of General George H. Thomas*

*Fight For Freedom: The American Revolutionary War*
(for young adults)

*The Battle of Nashville: General George H. Thomas and the Most Decisive*
*Battle of the Civil War*
(for young adults)

*A Passion For Victory: The Story of the Olympics in Ancient and Early*
*Modern Times*
(for young adults)

*The Caliph's Splendor: Islam and the West in the Golden Age of Baghdad*

# Praise for Some of the Author's Other Books

**LABYRINTHS OF IRON: SUBWAYS IN HISTORY, MYTH, ART, TECHNOLOGY & WAR**

"An extraordinarily original work, by a mind of the first order… Fresh and significant."
—Lewis Mumford, winner of the National Book Award for *The City in History*

"A remarkably interesting work… lucid and vivid."
—*The New Yorker*

"A work of welcome oddity and wit…with surprising information on almost every page… by a writer of original mind and pertinacious curiosity."
—*Newsweek*

"An unusual and captivating history, by a poet and gifted writer."
—*Publisher's Weekly*

**FEARFUL MAJESTY: THE LIFE AND REIGN OF IVAN THE TERRIBLE**

"The most objective and comprehensive analysis of Ivan which has ever appeared in English…A fresh interpretation."
—History Book Club, *History Book Club News*

"A lively portrait of Ivan the Terrible as a figure of high tragedy.
—*The New York Times Book Review*

"A powerful biography."
—*Atlanta Journal-Constitution*

**EAST OF THE SUN: THE EPIC CONQUEST AND TRAGIC HISTORY OF SIBERIA**

"Magnificent detail, meticulous research… Bobrick's thoughtful and comprehensive book… will reward any reader."
—*The Wall Street Journal*

"A panoramic history of Siberia that brims with interesting anecdotes and insights… Impressive."

# CONTENTS

| | |
|---|---|
| *Longfellow's "Sonnet 1"* | *13* |
| *Foreword* | *15* |
| *Acknowledgments* | *17* |
| Journey into Night, 1967 | 19 |
| Frost-Bite | 20 |
| The Way It Was | 21 |
| Negatives, Majorca, 1972 | 22 |
| The Search | 23 |
| Time out of Mind | 24 |
| He Chose to Part | 25 |
| An End to Innocence | 26 |
| The Nightwatchman | 28 |
| First Date | 29 |
| Palmistry | 30 |
| Doubt | 31 |
| To My Lover, on Christmas Day | 32 |
| Night | 33 |
| Taking Leave | 34 |
| Whatever the Weather | 35 |
| Mimesis | 36 |
| High & Low, 1991 | 37 |
| On a Day Becoming Clear | 38 |
| Meditation on the Rings | 39 |
| My Wife (A Singer) & I Go Down the Road, 1977 | 40 |
| Where the Rain Is Sweet | 41 |
| Mullein Flowers | 42 |
| Vignette | 43 |
| Love's Specific | 44 |
| A Colloquy of 3 Epigrams | |
| 1.    On Venus Having Her Exaltation in Pisces | 45 |
| 2.    A Sin Each Year | 46 |
| 3.    To My Books | 47 |
| Landseer's Lions | 48 |
| Eve's Lament | 49 |
| Epitaph | 50 |

The Strait of Messina                                      51
Wishbone                                                   52
Late Days                                                  53
The Archer                                                 54
Three Epigrams on Art
1.        How It Is                                        55
2.        To an Unfinished Poem                            56
3.        On Craft & Inspiration                           57
Two                                                        58
To My Muse                                                 59
The Language of Water                                      60
Photograph of Herman Melville                              61
Caedmon                                                    62
Unurned Burial                                             63
The Ecstasy of Connection                                 65
Scel Lem Duib                                              66
Vermont Spring                                             68
The Furnished Room                                         69
In an Antique Strain                                       71
Samson                                                     73
Requiem: For the Innocents                                 75
Made in America                                            76
Markab                                                     77
*Biographical Note*                                        *79*

*"These are strange times in which to practice such ancient austerities."*
—George Rochberg, letter to the author, May 15, 1997

*For Hilary, forever*
*&*
*Jim, who showed the way*

# HENRY WADSWORTH LONGFELLOW, SONNET 1 ON *THE DIVINE COMEDY*

Oft have I seen at some cathedral door
    A laborer, pausing in the dust and heat,
    Lay down his burden, and with reverent feet
    Enter, and cross himself, and on the floor
Kneel to repeat his paternoster o'er;
    Far off the noises of the world retreat;
    The loud vociferations of the street
    Become an undistinguishable roar.
So, as I enter here from day to day,
    And leave my burden at this minster gate,
    Kneeling in prayer, and not ashamed to pray,
    The tumult of the time disconsolate
To inarticulate murmurs dies away,
While the eternal ages watch and wait.

# FOREWORD

Long before my professional life as a writer began, the poet Muriel Rukeyser (whose son, Bill, was my friend at school) encouraged my earliest poetic efforts, as did my high school Humanities teacher and wrestling coach, Hagop Merjian, a poet versed in the poetry of many lands. Edward W. Tayler, the great Renaissance scholar, mentor, and later friend, broadened my horizons still further during (and after) my university years. Another great friend and mentor, P.L. Travers (herself the student of A.E. and Yeats) exhorted me to persevere. As this volume took shape, Rachel Hadas took time out from her duties as poetry editor of *The Classical Outlook* to give some poems a careful reading, with practical advice about modern conventions; Martin Elster read them through with his inimitable eye for form. But my greatest debt by far is to my eldest brother, Jim, himself an accomplished poet, whose profound knowledge of poetic tradition trained up my ear from a very early age. Inspired by his example, I studied Latin and Greek, wrote Latin epigrams in college to better grasp the subtle mysteries of meter and elision, and steeped myself in the great English poets from Chaucer to Auden, and beyond. His sense and sensibility, in certain ways, schooled my own; and though we are both now old and gray with years, he remains the reader over my shoulder I most rely on still.

The 53 poems included in this volume were written over the course of five and a half decades. Some date to my twenties and early thirties, before my first narrative history, *Labyrinths of Iron*, was published in 1981. Thereafter my writing life and livelihood were largely given over to the fourteen histories I would write during the next thirty-five years. Yet poetry was ever the soul of my world, and I gave the same exacting care, craft, and devotion to my poems as I did to my prose. My taste in poetic form has always been formal, and it never occurred to me to express myself in any other way, as my own natural voice seemed to favor traditional forms. Yet it is only by adapting the old to the new that language lives. It is, in any case, my unshakeable conviction that well-wrought work, inspired by true insight and feeling, is not the plaything of time or fashion, but belongs to the life of poetry itself. In arranging the poems, I have not adhered strictly to their chronology, but deliberately mingled them for counterpoint and theme. A few early poems, however, have dates attached.

A Biographical Note is appended to the end of this book.

October 8, 2025
Brattleboro, VT

# ACKNOWLEDGEMENTS

I am most grateful to the editors of the following publications where my poems have thus far been accepted or appeared:

*Blue Unicorn:* "On Craft & Inspiration," "To an Unfinished Poem," "How It Is," and "Landseer's Lions"
*Parabola*: "Whatever the Weather"
*Arion: A Journal of Humanities and the Classics,* "Requiem: For the Innocents"
*The Chesterton Review:* "The Nightwatchman," "Night," and "Mimesis"
*Stand: The Poetry Journal of the University of Leeds,* "Palmistry," "The Language of Water," and "Markab"
*Sparks of Calliope*: "My Wife (A Singer) & I Go Down the Road" and "Doubt"
*The Seventh Quarry Poetry Journal:* "Caedmon," "The Search," "Journey into Night, 1967," and "Taking Leave"
*Mediterranean Poetry*: "The Strait of Messina"
*The Pennsylvania Literary Journal*: "On A Day Becoming Clear," "Two," "Frost-Bite," "To My Muse: Before A Reading of Anna Akhmatova's Poems, March 5, 1998," "Mullein Flowers," and "Negatives, Majorca, 1972"
*Pulsebeat Poetry Journal*: "The Archer"
*The Penwood Review:* "To My Lover, On Christmas Day"
*Marble Poetry Magazine:* "Meditation on the Rings"
*The Madrid Review*: "Vignette"
*The Orchards Poetry Journal:* "Wishbone"
*The Galway Review:* "He Chose to Part," "A Colloquy of 3 Epigrams": "On Venus Having Her Exaltation in Pisces," "A Sin Each Year," "To My Books," and "Scel Lem Duib," translation.
*Orbis International Quarterly:* "Samson"
*The Frogmore Papers:* "Photograph of Herman Melville in Old Age"
*North Dakota Quarterly:* "Epitaph"

# JOURNEY INTO NIGHT, 1967

I wonder at my place among these lives—
the Brooklyn to Manhattan train
stammering the darkness, speech
lost to the coherent, simple sleep
of other men.  I wonder at these eyes
like dusk before me in this subway dawn,
what secrets of disaster each pair hides,
what words, like mine, unspoken, each had wished to say—
on this, the last-mile shuttle of their longest day.
How many times, perhaps, such eyes betrayed
their own mute longing for the one they loved
with downcast looks of diffidence or shame.
Now tired, staring at the ads above,
these people are all haunted by their names.

# FROST-BITE

Sometimes when I'm feeling just too tired
for pushing off again across the ice,
for all the rest there is in after-gliding
(which is the rest of pleasure from desire)
and yet I'm not quite ready to get off,
I've tried to rest a while by standing still
and balancing myself by shifts aloft,
because the slightest wind turns you at will
and makes you go contrarily by notions—
I've found, then, though grown expert at device,
a strong gust of wind still sends you sliding,
whether because the blades are curved for motion,
or because the gravity of our weight
works against us, you can't stand still on skates
for long without them scattering underneath,
which takes more out of you than anything,
unless it is the harm that comes from falling,
or what it takes to get back on your feet.

# THE WAY IT WAS

I wrote a poem out once without thought—
it was a haul of scattered things I'd caught
somewhere in me somehow like a net.
I was the only reason they'd connect.
I think there was emotion in their drag.
Commotion anyway (from all the snags).
That happens when your lines have too much lag.

# NEGATIVES,
# MAJORCA, 1972

I hold the negatives against the light—
your continental tan, born
in France, darkened in Spain,
too perfect for the lens to photograph,
and yet (like something known by half)
with a mask-like pallor worn,
from its reversal to my sight—
a face now foreign in a foreign land.

So many years have passed since I remained
baffled and distraught upon that strand.
Did you choose well to give up what we had?
There is in us an opposite suborned
by how we would be seen in love and known—
an unseen self, with longings we retain,
like some indelible emulsion stain—
as we divide, and subdivide, our paths.

For that, in time, our whole lives must atone.

Tonight I hold my face up to the light,
as if you were here still.  Now sand
fills with ocean in Majorca.  Night
quickens the silvered mirror with your face,
then mine, and both are clearer now and bright
with each familiar feature I can trace
with more than I can hope to understand.

# THE SEARCH

My soul lived in a city I had seen
in post-war newsreels, in black and white.
In one interchangeably repeated frieze,
the buildings were in rubble.  Refugees
hurried without hope across the screen,
while something harshly blanched about the light
betrayed the day's decline in every scene.

In a gray doorway somewhere, or a room,
two desperate lovers had been trying to meet.
It didn't matter since their love was doomed—
either by some act of the police,
whose power for malice was assumed,
or their own futile efforts in defeat.

And so it was, that during my younger years,
out of an early loss, I made an idol of my fears.

# TIME OUT OF MIND

(Or, Love's Anxiety)


For you, I know, that March time passed
smooth as sand in an inverted glass,
or regularly beat out its tick and tock
by the rudimentary hours of the clock.

But in those same days I lived through
whole seasons of reversal.  March
was a month through which December blew,
when blistering August heat could parch
the eve of a night Mayflowers grew.

Time was like a tempest and a sea.
It pounded the sand so finely,
and coarsely rolled great boulders toward the shore,
where after something like eternity,
they would be ground to sand, and nothing more.

# HE CHOSE TO PART

He chose to part.  Alone in his new place,
he sought to set things up his own way.  All
the furniture he set against the walls
to open up an airy middle space
(for wasn't it more breathing space he'd sought?)

His solitude, now reinforced around,
freed him to himself.  Even so, he found
how much also of emptiness he'd wrought.

# AN END TO INNOCENCE

When I was nine
a Talmudic sage*
bowed low to shake my hand.
From out of the
cinder-scarred world
of his family's persecuted past,
here was a towering man,
with a kindly face,
bright twinkling eyes and beard,
freed by some timeless
wisdom from his fear
of all things darkened
in the human race.

A friend to great
and mighty men
in the gnarled Affairs
of Church and State,
privy to the inmost lies
of those unseeing
what they know and see,
yet: hating no one
in a world of hate,
he said, "Your
grandfather told me
you were a student here.  So I
wanted to say, 'Hello.'"

It was *I* in my
fearful shyness then,
so moved by instinct
by his kindly grace

that, for a moment,
hid my stricken face,
not wanting to offend,
and shed an anguished tear.*

---

*      Rabbi Louis Finkelstein, then head of the Jewish Theological Seminary of America. He was a close friend of my grandfather, a Methodist Bishop. I was in boarding school at the time, where I had been sent after my mother died when I was 8.

# THE NIGHTWATCHMAN

He was like their conscience—how they spent
their time at night, with whom they came and went,
or if alone, their dark-entrusted states
were shown him with misgiving where he'd wait.

Though he was hired for them, and they his charge,
as things are reckoned at the going rate,
they felt they paid enough for him in rent,
which reckoned up, the tips were never large.

# FIRST DATE

After a day of waiting without measure,
the dinner lasted far into the night,
yet: we ate almost nothing: just enough
to bridge the silences in conversation—

for Time for us, by one barometer of love,
was like the stillness of impending weather,
hovering somewhere with suspended might—

but towards the end we made this resolution:
sometime to sit down to write together
a poem, line by line, each other taking
turns, not caring if it turned out rough,

for we knew when we swore that undertaking—
though jarring storms might one day form above—
a certain harmony was in the making,

and in the end the lines would rhyme enough.

# PALMISTRY

You slept, and in your sleep I took your hand,
palm to palm, so that our life lines joined,
and all our mounts were molded to one plain.

Would I could take the imprint of your fate
into my own flesh, as by a brand,
that all our turnings might turn out the same.

# DOUBT

I am no longer confident of culmination—
the voice of Truth, the Protean voice of forms
languishing responsive to elation,
is like a youth held fast with fascination
in an old man's arms.

# TO MY LOVER, ON CHRISTMAS DAY

When I woke this morning
and I thought of you,
more than ever in my life
I was grateful for this day,
past all the gifts that have been given,
and taken, in their time, away,
this: to be at last forgiven,
not just by what your words could say,
but on this fleshed, incarnate day
of Love transfigured without end,
you took me in your arms again.

# NIGHT

I had to get out of my room and walk.
I walked to where even late the streets
are not so desolate one might not meet
on an outside chance, someone and talk.

Shadows thrown by lamplight from the curbs
merged indifferently from gray to black.
I sought in phantom faces, looking back,
the still promise of one reassuring word.

But something in my purpose was not true.
Strangers passing strangers turn aside
in fear, in dark estrangement, or in pride.
I must have been looking for someone I knew.

# TAKING LEAVE

When we had stayed together for a while,
and all our things were thrown together too,
I missed the things that held my solitude,
borne back upon the years now, mile by mile.

By careless mingling, we had left no room
for growth, as we would say—but it was true:
by lusting after passion's absolutes,
with which the byways of our love were strewn,

what we had cherished most had then despised
as haunting specters of our desperate need
from which in tears we struggled to be free,
which turned our absolutions into lies.

Yet now that we are going separate ways,
the packs upon my back would weigh me down,
and I would almost lay them down, and stay,
did I not have to bear them for my own.

# WHATEVER THE WEATHER

(For P.L. Travers)


Whatever the weather, let it be extreme:
let the sun bake out of me the dross,
the rain come down in sheets and wash
me through, the wind blow through my seams.

Let nothing of me remain but what
innately is, archaic, seer,
a glass in which, as in a crystal sphere,
the whirl-wind-water-fire are caught.

# MIMESIS

There is a God and He is watching this
small act of homage to His greater power,
trying my poor hand at creation,
hour after hour after hour—
dare I even call it recreation,
when even by that word I am remiss?

# HIGH & LOW, 1991

*"The literature of individuals is a human product. The divine art is the story, with luminous characters on a higher plane. You may well be afraid of them."*
—Isak Dinesen


Time was, the drama of our humble lives,
married to art, would celebrate
the timeless tales and mysteries
of things divine. In that sacred shrine,
artists strove to venerate,
not the private meanings we assign
to our own joys and miseries—
however wrought, or overwrought, our states—
but archetypes, eternal in design:

So I have resolved, for better or worse,
that whatever I write inspired by you,
you will not see: I will not rehearse
seduction here. Whatever I do
in life, must have some sanctuary
somewhere from itself. In art,
I cannot deny the contrary,
delphic divinations of the heart.

# ON A DAY BECOMING CLEAR

It was good to hear the rain at last come down.
All morning long I'd waited for the mist
to lift.  The way it hung off from the ground,
as if its weight were something to resist,
made clearing seem what morning was about.

But I had also felt its weight in doubt.
And feeling, too, it might not be got around,
I was almost as glad to hear it insist—
like something that had come into its own—
at last, as to have had the sun come out.

# MEDITATION ON THE RINGS

Jade, a vulnerable stone,
is not like the rigid diamond, hard;
nor does it show its light in spires
of fiery dispersion, like a star.
Its earthly wear is shown
more in its ambiguities of tone,
in that deep green that emperors admired,
and, often, in its scars.

When wear is rough,
sometimes a sudden shock
of no great strength's enough
to cleave a diamond through.
Jade's tectonic core is tough,
its crystals interlock
and cleave together true:
it is the toughest rock.

# MY WIFE (A SINGER) & I
# GO DOWN THE ROAD, 1977

Blest pair of Sirens, Voice & Verse,
keep the hollow from our purse,
now that we have put you first;

Give us both enough to eat,
shoes below to clothe our feet,
rafters up above from sleet;

Tea and honey for the throat,
pen and paper for the notes,
and the lines for which I hope.

# WHERE THE RAIN IS SWEET

Wherever you are, my home is—
there holly grows, and the rain is sweet,
and Christmas comes with every kiss
beneath love's green immortal wreath.

Here is a wreath of mistletoe
twined round with holly, bearing red,
leaf berries. With the white they show
that when in life the wine and bread
of joy and sacrifice are shared
(however else true love is fed)
and simple grace and passion paired
with love upon the marriage bed,
home is an embodied prayer.

Wherever you are, my home is—
there holly grows, and the rain is sweet,
and Christmas comes with every kiss
beneath love's green immortal wreath.

# MULLEIN FLOWERS

Called common now, the mullein grows
a long way from its first Garden's keep.
It is the wild flower of our meadows.
Its golden blossoms open to the heat
of August, on the long spikes of its stalks.
Its fabled leaves are soft as any fleece.

No one knows from where it was first brought—
from Sicily, Tunisia, or Greece,
or some place else now almost out of thought—
But annals show, before its vast increase,
its entrance into History was cleaved
by fire—Romans, from the shorn stalks,
made torches for their funerals; the Greeks,
to light their studies, lamp-wicks from the leaves.

# VIGNETTE

On the corner, a loitering pimp
clutched at his ten-gallon hat.
A kind of arthritic shuffle
brought him to a door
from where, leaning limp-
ly on a gold-tipped cane,
he ruled his rude domain
of the rank and rankly used,
in suave decrepitude.

# LOVE'S SPECIFIC

(A Nominalist on Love)


Today you caught me looking at you wanting.
I haven't a thing to say in my defense.
Your sleave-silk yellow hair combed down in curls
to swirl about your neck, your negligence
in speech, its shy come-hither classic taunting,
your small breasts tipped up in eminence.
You are like some Idea of the World.
But I don't know if who you are is true.

And yet I know—as all of us must—too:
our own true loves will have particular eyes,
they'll see us, too, not quite as we are, yet wanting,
for all the ideas they may have of me, or you,
a particular knowledge of our lies.

# A COLLOQUY OF 3 EPIGRAMS

## 1. ON VENUS HAVING HER EXALTATION IN PISCES

Astrologers, mark well my birth,
the Ides of March, its double curse:
that whom I most love will betray
my love, yet love blind all my days.

## 2. A SIN EACH YEAR

A sin each year was punished in me when
I went away to boarding school for ten:
that made the Decalogue: before I came
to sinning as a man, I knew the shame.

# 3. TO MY BOOKS

(for Edward W. Tayler)


You, who have willed my good,
always the best of friends,
I have, as best I could,
willed yours, by my amends.

# LANDSEER'S LIONS*

The lions in Trafalgar Square
have a colonial stare;
the eyes of the English, too,
a far-away hue—

imbued with ebbing memories, yet aware
of having once been everywhere,
now, in another time, they look at you
from landlocked hemispheres of ruined blue.

*      Bronze castings, designed by Sir Edwin Landseer and installed in 1868, to commemorate the naval victory of Horatio Nelson in 1805 over the Spanish and French fleets.

# EVE'S LAMENT

*"It was from out the rind of one apple tasted, that the knowledge of good and evil, as two twins cleaving together, leapt forth into the world."*
—John Milton, *Areopagitica*


It was as if you gave me life itself,
or brought me back to life, that early spring,
when summer came, I thought of nothing else
but that sweet fruit that made my palate sting.

You were the very marrow of my bones,
the redness of my blood and in the light,
the body of the shadow that I cast,
a crystalline refraction of my sight.

When you had gone, I vanished in thin air
as if a nothingness had come to pass,
every mirror was transparent glass
through which an absence stared.

I am bound to you by more than blood,
more subtle than the subtleties of kind,
of the one apple tasted, that's the rind,
however halved the skin and flesh for food—

a knowledge drawn, from that accursed tree,
of opposites dissevered and combined,
from our shared appetite: that made you mine,
and a God-forsaken villain out of me.

# EPITAPH

As many poems as tonight I started
died in my hands—I almost said my arms—
I could not go away so heavy-hearted,
so stirred after the glimmerings of their charms,
without some word, if only in alarm,
of memorial, for what had been martyred.

# THE STRAIT OF MESSINA

"Spiritual passivity is an invitation to Evil."
—Yvor Winters


A day as well for the draining.  Rain
off and on.  A rock-gray lay of light.
Nothing seeming to mean much in the main.
Can one ever say this and be right?

The vagueness of the opposite lying shores
stirred in me nothing like thirst or hunger.
The voyage was idle and under
No peril: there was nothing it was for.

Oh, there was nothing in me to resist
the stir of feelings nothing yet could phrase
as warning, out of the mist's implicit hiss
and the fog-horn's dog-like baying through the haze.

# WISHBONE

That we might know the symmetry of fate,
and what the Almighty Architect requires
in recognition of our humble state,
he gave this emblematic bone its shape—
its Gothic-arch-like niche and spire
        as recess to the heart's desire,
but for one fatal weakness in its make:
each end belies whichever end we take,
the long equalities of our mistakes
make up the long and short of our desires,
        whichever way our wishes break.

# LATE DAYS

(from Horace, *Satires,* II.6, lines 1-5)

This is what I prayed for: a modest piece of land,
with a garden near the house, and a never-failing spring—
some woodlands, too—this much and more
the gods have granted, beyond anything
I could have hoped for (given my poor past)
from Fortune's fitful hand.  May these blessings last!


(Hoc erat in votis: modus agri non ita magnus,
hortus ubi et tecto vicinus iugis aquae fons
et paulum silvae super his foret. auctius atque
Di melius fecere. bene est. nil amplius oro,
Maia nate, nisi ut propria haec mihi munera faxis.)

# THE ARCHER

He bent his bow till both ends met
just in a circle at his ear,
then shot: the arrow sang: it set
its course aloft into the black
and million starry spangled sphere.
Up, up it sang, its perfect track
was straight, toward what fixed star it flew
or falling star, its head appeared
(though who could follow it were few)
a star itself to our rapt view.

But he, soon as that shaft came clear,
stripped straight-grained branches from the yew
for arrows with the surest cut,
and fitted them against his ear,
and hitched his sacred quiver up.

## THREE EPIGRAMS ON ART

## 1.   HOW IT IS

If something isn't, by Creation, in you,
as sinuosity in sinew,
you can't acquire its Virtue from without—
though virtuosity may come about.

## 2.   TO AN UNFINISHED POEM

A jug of wine, a loaf of bread, and thou
increasing, line by line, upon my brow.

# 3.   ON CRAFT & INSPIRATION

For every four-line epigram I write,
I scotch four lines at least to get it tight.
It takes a fifth of Scotch to get it right.

# TWO

Straight from my side and warm you curled
in sudden coldness from my reach.
I felt your strangeness inward whirl
into your own revolving world,
and heard, in your remotest speech,
the hollow echo in the breach
of seven sundered planets hurled
into their own orbits, each to each—

and yet, you had but turned to sleep.

# TO MY MUSE: BEFORE A READING OF ANNA AKHMATOVA'S POEMS, BRATTLEBORO, VT, MARCH 5, 1998

How long has it been since I was moved to write
a poem to a lover: is not this of the soul?
And that farewell, during one of the White Nights
of St. Petersburg, was nine long years ago.

Now here in Vermont the sun is setting
slowly over the hills: the falling light still glows,
and I, awakening to my Self and you—
the wound of absence closing, and forgetting,
even by this number, weight, and rhyme—
all that matters is that I see you tomorrow.
Light splashes on my page like iodine.

# THE LANGUAGE OF WATER

(To a poet overwhelmed by emotion)


*The language of water, seething*
*in the white recessions of the surf,*
for you, drawn ever in and massing
to fall in breakers to the earth;

unloosed in all its tidal force
from the given margins of the land,
to swell with all the feeling of its source
in all the forms that feeling can demand—

only to have its thinned, rescinded voice
spend itself like spindrift in the sand.

# PHOTOGRAPH OF HERMAN MELVILLE IN OLD AGE

His face was creased, but set
as though in a mold; his hair,
brushed back severely from his brow,
brought the broad blunt forehead forward
like a mass of stone.  Beneath that ridge,
his two eyes lived in caves.  A dark line
marked his mouth, his beard,
swept down, was gray and thick,
and dense with years,
yet squarely cropped
like a privet hedge with shears.

His was a face like Time itself,
by Will and Fate approved,
beyond all love and hate,
unmoving, and unmoved.

# CAEDMON*

Of words, and the murder of words, he dreamed,
whose very syllables were the sounds of fears.
No utterance could be counted on to clear
the barrier of his breath that teemed
with forced occlusions mingled with his tears,
until an angel came and touched his tongue,
and all he ever yearned to say, was sung,
that we might know the glories that we live among.

---

*    A 7th century Anglo-Saxon lad who stammered badly, until an angel
released him from his affliction. Then, he burst forth in hymns to the cre-
ation of the world.

# UNURNED BURIAL

All the faces were sober
and the right words were said,
as the company gathered
to part with the dead.

The priest took the ashes
in handfuls and placed
each one in just portion
with something like grace
about the church garden
with its wild ivy wall,
though clouds had begun
to shadow the knoll
and the hour was chased
by the sun in its fall.

But Time's fateful limit
soon weighed on the priest,
who mindful of minutes,
and eager to finish,
forgot the deceased.
With growing dispersions,
she emptied the urn,
till in one uncouth gesture,
as if in disdain,
she dumped by a stump
all that remained.

Oh, do not to me
as she did to him,
hasten me gone
on some callous whim.
Let your hands be calm,
deliberate, poised.
Pause for a psalm.
Quiet all noise,
as if my still dust
held now in your palm
in spirit still throbbed
with sorrows and joys.

Think me not unworthy of the prize
of heaven—nor yet, contrariwise,
that you are bound to join the blessed host.
For on the Day when we may rearise
from dust to us, to our immense surprise,
your careless handling of one lowly ghost,
though it might seem inconsequent to most,
might yet be viewed above with burning eyes,
by One annoyed, and make you toast.

# THE ECSTASY OF CONNECTION

(Or, The Art of Poetry & Life)


Punctuality is the soul of wit—
not being early, and wasting time;
not being late.  The right word
at the right time: time into space:
the right word in the right place.
Everything in its season.  Proportion,
in life, in art.  That which rhymes,
with tempered meter, sings,
as in our lives, the whole of it,
with virtues tempering our sins,
our hearts and minds united with our ears,
in cosmic harmony to that which spins,
that we might hear, what seldom yet was heard
in revelations of the Word:
a singing flinging from the turning spheres!

# SCEL LEM DUIB*

Oh, my news is poor:
stags roar;
winter descends;
summer ends;

cold high blasts;
a low sun
on a short run;
sea fast.

Bracken rigid,
reddening;
overhead
wild geese crying.

Cold has iced
the wings of birds.
Death in life.
That's the word!

---

* Translation of an Old Irish Poem, ca. 9th century. An early draft appeared under a pseudonym in *Ais-Eiri*, the magazine of the Irish Arts Center in New York, in 1978. The original is given after the translation.

Scél lem dúib:
   dordaid dam;
snigid gaim:
   ro fáith sam:

Gáeth ard úar;
   ísel grían;
gair a rrith;
   ruirthech rían;

Rorúad rath;
   ro cleth cruth;
ro gab gnáth
   giugrann guth.

Ro gab úacht
   etti én;aigre ré;
   é mo scél.

# VERMONT SPRING

When late you tapped the sweet sap from the tree
in budding time, up from the thawing root,
you took the milky stream, and what accrued—
boiling off the bounty into steam—
made syrup pure—almost more than true:
for you could taste the fire in it, too.

# AFTER THE FALL:
# THE FURNISHED ROOM

The bracelet he wore, from an unknown time,
was tricked with roughly hammered cups
inset with beads of serpentine.

Its cord-like central twist of wire
of tarnished metal left a mark
of blackened sulfur on his wrist,
as if it wrapped his wrist in fire.

"Its crudeness draws me," he said,
as she drew him toward the bed.

When they made love, it was like
an act of idolatry.  They fed
upon each other like fruit—or, like
fresh slicked clay on the potter's wheel,
molded each other anew with their hands.
It was, for them, as like the Promised Land
as anything they ever hoped to know,
at once chimerical and real,
and as they liked it, taken fast or slow,
he felt, by their complete exchange,
his very life that day drawn forth,
towards some unfathomably
warm succulent place in her womb
to which his ache and force
were umbilically tied.
                 Yet afterwards,
the furnished room
seemed merely commonplace and strange,
now readied for some other guests,

in whom the lust for life in joy and shame
would either be exalted or confessed.

# IN AN ANTIQUE STRAIN*

"Truth did not come into the world naked, but in 'types' and images. One cannot receive the Truth in any other way."
—*The Gospel of Philip,* ca. 250 C.E.

Once upon a time, instead of Nature
with its enumerated Laws,
there was Wonder with a Will.
The Gods drove their flocks across the sky
through a woven tapestry of shining clouds,
and when the fabled flocks had grazed their fill,
the clustered herds would pause
to shake their moist fleece out upon the earth
in gentle showers and cascades of rain.
And sometimes in their anger, or their mirth,
the Gods in their councils would grow loud
(for all the Gods were nothing if not proud)
and reasoning from spite or mighty pride,
by which they moralized the ways of Fate,
distribute joys and sorrows through the world.
And all the wandering planets and the stars
in storied constellations, and the tales
of striving heroes, profligate or wise,
or both (not knowing yet) and setting sail
into new worlds, stupendous to their eyes,
of unimagined chances near and far—
for love or lust, conquest, peace, and war—
with only heaven's mystic grace to guide
their odyssey to where safe harbors are:
Each by nature choosing their own path—
Achilles, sullen in his tent with wrath,
Icarus fallen headlong from his pride,

---

\*     With a nod to John Fiske's *Myths and Myth-Makers* (1872).

the lust of Phaedra and of Pasiphae,
as monstrous, both, as Minos in his greed,
Ixion bound forever to his wheel
of fire.  Niobe, weeping, turned to stone.
Among them all, Odysseus alone,
ordained by fate to a fate more blessed,
tempted by all that we might know and feel,
yet paying the errant price he owed,
returned at last to his night-ravaged home—
the Solar Hero with unerring bow.

And so the Sun God, flaming ever west
urged his golden chariot through the sky
in one sure arc, until at eventide,
he met, in violet light, his twilight bride,
just where the far horizon meets the sea,
and there each day his love renewed the dawn,
vanquishing the devils of the night,
and, by his rising, righting every wrong.

All these, on their elevated plain,
told us the stories of our own fraught lives,
not by the transient pantomime of seems,
but by essential features—lost or gained,
that by the pattern of their tell-tale signs,
we might see, and know, and be redeemed.

Our lives are lived in fabled paradigms.

# SAMSON

(Adopted: 11/24/2020)


As much of a child as I shall ever know,
and care for, with all the devotion that I have,
the one I think of, when I hear lullabies,
ever since we took you home that day,
our car superfluously arrayed
with every kind of thing new parents buy,
wrapped in a blanket like swaddling clothes
against the chill of fall.  We knew,
having at last adopted you,
our elder lives would never be the same.
We named you then: you grew into your name,
larger than your parents might have thought,
had they had any thoughts about your size.
But as for us, we doted on your eyes,
and nose, and teeth, wanting you to be
as happily robust as any child
on whom devoted older parents thrive.
There were some challenges at first of course
in getting you to learn some do's and don'ts,
but in the end we accepted, as by law,
some things we'd always hoped you would, but won't.
You are yourself. When I would discuss
some matter with you, you look merely blank,
or questioning.  Or turn querulous.
So now that I am growing old,
this is perhaps the last chance I may have
to prove, however late, that I deserved
the pure devotion you have shown to me,
in all your helplessness and need,
along with some peremptory demands,

made on the assumption I was there
for no other reason than your care.
Each day you manifest that zest for life
that we all long for.  Of that I am in awe.
I think of things like these, and many more,
as you lie on a pillow on my knees,
stretched out, as so often, just because
you simply want to be with me,
and rest on me your little head and paws.

# REQUIEM: FOR THE INNOCENTS

*ὅτι εἰ ἐν τῷ ὑγρῷ ξύλῳ ταῦτα ποιοῦσιν,*
*ἐν τῷ ξηρῷ τί γένηται…*
—Luke 23:31

There are some things that must not be denied—
the heart sinks more than one had thought it could,
the mind loses its bearings to go by,
invoke whom you will to condone it from on high—
*if they would do this in the green wood,*
*what may happen in the dry?*

Merciful God, it must be testified,
from Rachel in Ramah, who wept hard tears
for all the children of Jerusalem—
which, some say, also prophesied
Herod, and those who would out-Herod him,
in time, killing the innocents they would,
from the ghettos of Europe to Gaza,
to the skulled mound where the True Cross stood—
there must not be a world of passers-by.
We know that one Samaritan was good.
*If they would do this in the green wood,*
*what may happen in the dry?*

Yet there is One, we hope, who hears their cries,
who died for them and for our brotherhood.
Let no one say it can be justified—
you cannot cut a cumin seed with God!
*If they would do this in the green wood,*
*what may happen in the dry?*

# MADE IN AMERICA

(November 5, 2024)


His cellmate was a large, brawny man
with a neck as thick as a tree trunk,
and a torso, where an involved code
of tattoos was fearsomely displayed.
Over the top of his shorn head,
a huge spider crawled across a web
that reached down to his brow; his back
was spanned by an onion-domed church,
set in a bleak subarctic stand of birch,
while across the lids of his closed eyes,
"Wake me not!" was stained in jagged lines.

The two domes of the church stood for
the number of times the man had been
imprisoned; the spider for
his lethal life of drug-related crimes.
A black-and-white diamond on his chest
proclaimed his sentence: fifty years to life.

All this he had arranged to imprint on himself,
with the help of a fellow inmate, from a dye
made from his own urine mixed with ash,
by means of an electric shaver joined
to a needle-tipped syringe jury-rigged
into a tattooing machine.
       Oh, this
was not the America we hoped for,
was it?  Or what we thought we knew.
But, Voter, I tell you true,
that cell and its companion are now yours,
and that inmate, You.

# MARKAB*

(An astrological poem)


Low in the sky, as evening falls,
a radiant, blue-white spectral star
rises in the east as summer ends.
It is a sign of autumn and portends
for some, whose Sun conjoins it at their birth,
a life of unbridled passion and desire.

Born of dread Medusa's viscous blood—
with Pegasus—from her wild severed head,
mixed with the sea foam of his raging sire,
Poseidon, God of horses and the sea—
Was this, then, meant to be the fate for me?

Or: like winged Pegasus, instead
(as symbol of the soul aspiring) freed
from that thick muck in which it had been mired,
if yet in stages, also made to rise
by that same star, shouldering the wing,
to where my thirst, and every thirst, is quenched,
beyond the constellated skies,
by living water's ever-welling spring?

---

\* A prominent star, of ambiguous meaning, with significance for Classical, Medieval, and Renaissance astrology, in the constellation Pegasus, where the shoulder joins the wing.

# BIOGRAPHICAL NOTE

**B**ENSON BOBRICK earned his doctorate in English and Comparative Literature from Columbia University. His many books have been featured on the front page of *The New York Times Book Review*, widely praised in both academic and popular journals, and published in translation in over twelve lands. As a narrative historian, he has been called, by *The New York Times*, "perhaps the most interesting American historian writing today." In 2002, he also received the Literature Award of the American Academy of Arts and Letters. Two distinguished poets, Galway Kinnell and Robert Pinsky, served on the Award Committee that year. Its other members were: Horton Foote, Hortense Calisher, Ann Beattie, and Russell Banks. Recently, his poems, crafted over many years, have been accepted by numerous publications both here and abroad. He lives in Vermont.

www.ingramcontent.com/pod-product-compliance
Lightning Source LLC
Chambersburg PA
CBHW030711110426
R18122000001B/R181220PG42736CBX00003B/3